S0-DUI-225

My Best Friend
Elena Pappas

DELETE THIS BOOK
from Jerabek School Library

My Best Friend Elena Pappas

Meeting a Greek-American Family

Phyllis S. Yingling

Pictures by Tricia Zimic

Julian Messner New York

JERABEK ELEMENTARY SCHOOL
10050 AVENIDA MAGNIFICA
SAN DIEGO, CA 92131

Text copyright © 1986 by Phyllis S. Yingling
Illustrations © 1986 by Tricia Zimic

All rights reserved
including the right to reproduction
in whole or in part in any form

Published by Julian Messner,
A Division of Simon & Schuster, Inc.
Simon & Schuster Building
Rockefeller Center
1230 Avenue of the Americas
New York, New York 10020

JULIAN MESSNER and colophon are trademarks
of Simon & Schuster, Inc.

Manufactured in the United States of America
Design by Nina Tallarico

10 9 8 7 6 5 4 3 2 1

Library of Congress Cataloging in Publication Data

Yingling, Phyllis S.
    My best friend, Elena Pappas.

    Bibliography: p.
    Summary: A child learns about the Greek American
culture when she becomes friends with Elena Pappas and
shares family experiences.
    [1. Greek Americans—Fiction. 2. Friendship—Fiction]
I. Zimic, Tricia. II. Title.
PZ7.Y56My   1986   [Fic]   86-5310

ISBN: 0-671-62090-8

Acknowledgments

Many people have been helpful in preparing this book. I want to express my gratitude to: Harry and Nicki Sharkey, their daughters, Despina (Debbie) and Potoula (Peggy), and Nicki's mother, Mrs. Mary Maistros, for so graciously sharing their time and family traditions; to Father Constantine Monios and Father Louis Noplos for providing information about the Greek Orthodox Church and its role among Greek-American families; to Maria Nicolaidis-Karanikolas, Peter Maruda, Senator Paul Sarbanes, Alexander's Photographics, and the many others in Baltimore's Greek Community for their kindness and cooperation while I was gathering material for the book; to Linda Beck for typing the manuscript, and special thanks to my husband, Carroll, for his patience and encouragement, and for being an enthusiastic partner in research.

Contents

My Best Friend
Elena Pappas

❧ 1 ❧
A New Home and New Friends

When we moved from West Virginia to Baltimore, I left all my friends behind. On the day in November when we moved into our new house, Elena Pappas and her mother came over to visit. They live right next door. I didn't know it then, but Elena was going to be my new best friend.

Elena's family came from Greece. Their last name used to be Papadopoulos. I think that's fun to say. But now their name is Pappas.

Elena is in the same fourth grade class I'm in. On my first day at the new school we walked home together to her house. Her grandmother Pappas lives with them. She fixed us some milk and butter cookies called *koulourakia* (koo-luh-RAK-ee-a). Grandmother Pappas asked how I liked Baltimore and all. I told her about having to leave our big old house in West Virginia and how terribly I missed my best friend, Jenny, and all the other kids.

"Oh, my little *koukla!*" she said. "I know just how you feel. When I first came to the United States from Greece I cried for days." Grandmother Pappas is a tiny lady with short dark hair that's going gray. When she was young she must have looked like Elena . . . pretty and thin with beautiful black wavy hair. She took my hands in hers. "Lucy Dean, I will tell you about my journey to America.

"When I was fourteen years old, I lived with my mother and two younger brothers in a small village in Greece. My father had died three years before. One day, a letter came from my mother's brother, Uncle Spiro, who had moved to America ten years earlier. He had started a small business in New York City, selling Coney Island hot dogs. His business was so successful that now he had a big restaurant.

"In the letter he told about one of his waiters. He was a nice young man of twenty-five, my uncle said. He wanted to marry a Greek girl. In those days, it was mostly the men who left Greece to find work in the United States. There were few Greek women here. Uncle Spiro decided to play matchmaker." Grandmother smiled and sipped a cup of coffee. "So now, he was writing to my mother and telling her to get me on the next ship leaving Piraeus for New York. In the envelope was the money for my ticket."

"Were you glad to come to America?" I asked Grandmother Pappas.

"No, no, *koukla*," she said. "I loved my home. And I already had my eye on a young man in my village that I hoped to marry."

"Weren't you too young to get married?" asked Elena. "Why didn't your mother just write back and tell Uncle Spiro 'No'?"

"Oh, Elena," said her grandmother, "the old days were different. My mother was a widow. Her older brother was the head of the family. It was his place to help her find a husband for her only daughter. Fourteen was considered a good age for a girl to marry back then."

Grandmother Pappas got down from the stool and poured us some more milk. "In any case, it worked out for the best. In two weeks I was on a ship bound for New York. Uncle Spiro's money paid only for a ticket in steerage, the most crowded part of the ship. It wasn't exactly like sailing on the Queen Elizabeth." Grandmother laughed. "The trip lasted three weeks. During that time I was both seasick and homesick. I spent the time trying to imagine what New York would be like.

"It was the language difference that brought the first tears. I spoke only Greek, so when I arrived at Ellis Island I didn't understand one word that was said to me. Finally, I recognized Uncle Spiro in the crowd of people waiting on the other side of the barrier. I was so happy to see him, even though he was the cause of all my troubles. Tears of joy mixed with the tears of sorrow and anger that were already streaming down my face."

"Did you marry the man your uncle had in mind for you?" I asked.

Grandmother Pappas seemed surprised at the question. "Oh, yes, of course," she replied. "Soon after I arrived in New York, I met Alexandros. I was so shy I could hardly lift my eyes to look at him."

"Was he handsome? Did you love him?" I asked.

Grandmother Pappas smiled, though there were tears in her eyes. "Yes, he was very handsome. His hair was thick and black as a coal and he had a big moustache to match it." She reached over and touched Elena's arm. "He was your grandfather, *koukla*. He died shortly after you were born." She looked out the window and sighed. "Oh, yes. I learned to love him very much."

We were all quiet for a while. Then Mrs. Pappas laughed. "At first, he seemed to me so *old* and so *dull*. We were not allowed to see each other without a chaperone. When we were together we said very little. Once, before we were married, he took me to a dance at the Greek church hall. It was a lovely evening. There were people from many parts of Greece. They had brought their dances with them . . . and we danced them all. Since we were only engaged, Alexandros and I were not allowed even to hold hands. In the dancing we each had to hold on to a handkerchief between us."

"What would have happened if you had held hands?" Elena asked.

"The engagement would have been called off and my reputation would have been ruined." Grandmother Pappas was very serious now. "My mother always told me, 'A girl's reputation is like a beautiful dish. Once it is broken it may be possible to mend it, but it will never be quite the same.' "

"And so you got married and lived happily ever after, huh, *Yia Yia* (yah-YAH)?" said Elena.

"Yes, of course, *koukla*," laughed Mrs. Pappas. "After your father and his brothers were born there was never a dull moment." She smiled at me. "So, Lucy Dean, before you decide you don't like your new home, give it some time."

I smiled. Maybe, I thought to myself. Nice as Elena and Grandmother Pappas are, they're not the same as Jenny and my other friends. I just stood there trying to keep smiling as Grandmother Pappas held me close.

❧ 2 ❧
My Lucky Year

This year we went back to West Virginia for Christmas. I was so excited I could hardly stand it. I had so much to tell Jenny. But, you know what? I kept missing Elena. I wanted her to meet my family and friends.

On New Year's Eve we went over to the Pappas' house to celebrate both the New Year and Saint Basil's Day. Saint Basil was a bishop in the olden days who was always helping people. If a family had trouble and needed money desperately Saint Basil would bake a loaf of bread and put some coins in the dough. Then he'd leave the loaf on their doorstep. There are lots of stories about the nice things Saint Basil did for people. His special day is January first, so Greek families remember him when they have their New Year's party.

The evening with the Pappas family began with dinner of lamb and rice. A huge salad bowl was filled with tomatoes, lettuce, cucumbers, green peppers, onions, garlic, a cheese called feta, and loads of ripe olives. I finally got to eat as many olives as I wanted.

After dinner, the women all sat around in the living room and talked. Elena's father took my dad to the recreation room where all the men were playing cards. She and I played Uno with her cousins until just before midnight. Her cousin, Despina, just moved here from Greece with her family a few years ago. She is so quiet and shy. But Elena's other cousin, Tony, was born in this country. He is so funny. You never know what Tony will think of next! He just loves to tease people.

They both live in Highlandtown. That's a part of Baltimore where many Greek people live. I've been there with Elena to visit her grandparents. You can hear Greek being spoken everywhere . . . on the streets, in the stores, and especially at church. I'm always amazed to hear her mom speaking Greek so easily. I'm learning a little bit of Greek. Now when I see Elena's grandparents I say *"Kalimera,"* for good morning, or *"Kalispera,"* for good evening.

As it got closer to twelve o'clock, we all went to the dining room and gathered around the table. Greek families celebrate Saint Basil's Day with a special loaf of bread called *Vasilopita* (vah-seh-LO-pee-tah) or Saint Basil's Bread. As the bread is being made, a coin, wrapped in foil, is kneaded into the dough. At the party, the bread is cut, one slice at a time. The first slice goes to "the house" and is set aside in case an unexpected guest arrives. The next slice is given to the oldest person present. After that, each slice is given to the next oldest person, until everyone gets a piece. Somewhere in the loaf is that coin, and whoever gets it is supposed to have good luck the rest of the year.

At the stroke of twelve everyone cheered and hugged and kissed each other, just as people do all over the world on New Year's Eve. We toasted each other with *"Yassou* (YAH-soo)." Then Mrs. Pappas began cutting the bread and everyone waited to see who would get the lucky coin. Guess what! It was in my piece. Everybody clapped and shouted *"Kali tihi* (kah-LEE TEE-hee)" for good luck, and I felt tingly all over. Mrs. Pappas served desserts and more drinks. The men went back to their cards, and we switched from Uno to Clue.

When we were ready to leave I couldn't find my gloves . . . the new ones I got for Christmas. We were all looking around in the bedroom where the coats were, when Tony said, "I'll bet Kalikanzari (kah-lee-kan-ZAH-ree) got them."

"Kalikan . . . who?" I asked.

"Kalikanzari," Tony repeated. "He's this little guy . . . something like an elf . . . who lurks around the house this time of year doing sneaky things—like snitching gloves." Tony imitated a gnome crouching and tiptoeing out of the room.

"Come back here, Tony!" called Elena's older sister, Maria. "Nobody believes in Kalikanzari anymore."

Then she turned to me and explained, "That's just a folktale from Grandmother's village."

Tony leaned against the door. "No, he's real, Maria," he insisted, looking pretty impish himself. "Just because you're all grown up and getting married doesn't mean you know everything. I *personally* saw Kalikanzari. And he went thataway!" Tony dashed down the stairs two at a time. Maria and Elena, laughing and shouting, chased after him. I looked at Despina, who just grinned, so we followed the others. Tony stopped in front of the sofa. "I saw him with my own eyes. He was right here." He lifted the middle cushion. "What did I tell you? Here they are." Bowing politely, he handed me my gloves. "You see, your good luck is starting already."

"Oh, Tony," laughed Elena. "*You* hid them there."

Tony grinned and winked at me. "It was Kalikanzari. Honest!" Then he turned and ran toward the kitchen with all of us girls on his heels. Just then Dad called, "Come on, people. It'll soon be sunup. Happy New Year, everybody."

"Happy New Year, Kalikanzari," I shouted into the kitchen.

"Happy Saint Basil's Day," yelled Tony.

3
A Visit from Daphne

I think Daphne Constantine is the most beautiful woman I've ever seen. My mom is pretty and so is Mrs. Pappas, but Daphne is gorgeous! She looks like a famous movie star or television personality. Well, actually, that's what she is. She's a television reporter for a station in Athens, Greece. She is Mrs. Pappas' cousin, and she's come here to interview outstanding Greek-Americans. Yesterday she taped an interview with Maryland Senator Paul Sarbanes.

Elena asked Mrs. Day if Daphne could speak to our class in social studies. Today Daphne came and brought slides of Greece to show us. Daphne said Greece is a nation of contrasts. The first slide she showed was of the Parthenon (PAR-the-non). That's the huge white temple with lots of pillars you see on travel posters. It's high up above Athens, the capital of Greece. The temples of the gods were up high because that was the safest place.

Next, Daphne showed us slides of Athens. It has

modern government buildings and tall office and apartment buildings. And it's got traffic jams like any other big city. Daphne pointed out the building where her television studios are.

The soldiers who guard the government buildings wear old-fashioned uniforms with short skirts, long white stockings, and big tassles on their shoes. But the rest of the army wear uniforms like the ones we see in our country. Mrs. Day said that the Greek people had a democratic government thousands of years ago. The Founding Fathers of our country got many ideas for our government from the Greek writers.

We saw ancient outdoor theaters that were built over two thousand years ago. But if you want to go to a movie, there are movie theaters just like ours.

Daphne said that one of the biggest contrasts was between the cities, like Athens, and the villages. There are villages high in the mountains and on the many islands that are part of Greece. Daphne had gone to a tiny village on an island to do a TV special. She showed slides of the narrow streets that wind up the mountains like a maze. She said they were made that way to protect the village from the pirates who used to attack the towns. Donkeys go up and down those little streets carrying things in baskets on their backs.

Last of all, Daphne showed us beautiful slides of the beaches. I think I'd like to go to Greece some day. Maybe Daphne will invite Elena and me over for a visit. It doesn't hurt to dream.

4
Maria Gets Married

Today was the day Elena's sister, Maria, got married. Elena was a flower girl in the wedding. What a wonderful day it was! Mr. Pappas asked us to drive his uncle who had flown here from Florida to the wedding, so we got there early. This was my first visit to the Greek Cathedral. Sitting there in the huge church with the large icons and beautiful stained glass windows gave me a quiet feeling of being someplace very special. At the front of the church was a delicately carved wooden screen. Part of it was like a door that opened and I could see the altar behind it.

The organist began playing quiet music, and people began to take their seats. Most of the people around us were whispering in Greek. I had seen Elena's dress at her house so I could hardly wait to see her in it.

As the organist began playing the wedding march, bridesmaids and ushers walked slowly down the aisle. Then came the maid of honor, Maria's best friend, Peggy. She was followed by the ring bearer. The way he

looked in that tuxedo, you'd never guess that he was the same Tony who is always giving us a hard time. After Tony came Nicki, Maria's sponsor or *koumbara* (koom-BAH-ra). Elena had told me how important *koumbaras* are. They are responsible for helping out if there is trouble in the marriage. They will also be the godparents of the couple's first child. At last Elena came down the aisle. I couldn't believe how pretty she looked. She was carrying a basket of pink flowers to match her dress. As she went by our seat she gave us a big smile.

Finally, Maria and her father came down the aisle. In her white wedding gown and long lace train, Maria looked like an angel. Yesterday, when I was at their house she was so nervous about the wedding. Mr. Pappas told her not to worry. He said he'd make sure his "little girl" got down the aisle all right. Now he was the one who looked nervous. I knew he was going to miss having Maria around the house. He and Maria have always been very close.

When Maria and her father reached the table where the priest, her fiancé George, and the wedding party were waiting, Mr. Pappas lifted her veil and kissed her. Then the service began.

It seemed mysterious to me when the priest began chanting in Greek. Then he placed rings on the couple's fingers. After that, Harry, who was George's *koumbaro*, slipped the rings on the hands of the bride and groom three times. I found out Greeks wear their wedding rings on their right hands.

After the ring ceremony, the wedding began. The priest picked up two candles from the table, lit them, and gave Maria and George each a candle to hold. A man read from the Bible, and the priest chanted some prayers. Then the priest placed crowns of flowers on their heads, and the sponsors wove the crowns back and forth three times, from one head to another, to show that their lives are now together.

Later the priest took Maria's hand, Maria took George's arm, and Nicki held Maria's train off the floor. Harry held the two crowns on the couple's heads. All five of them walked around the table three times in a sort of dance. The priest was chanting, and Maria and George looked like they could float right off. It was such a happy time!

After a short talk, the priest kissed both Maria and George on both cheeks. That's what they do in Europe. Then the parents came up and kissed everybody, and that was it. Maria and George were married.

The wedding reception was in a large hotel. A band played Greek music. The wedding song, called *Oraia Nymphi* (ou-REH-ah NEE-fee), "How Beautiful the Bride," filled the room. George led Maria out onto the dance floor. Then the bride's parents, the groom's parents, their grandparents and brothers and sisters, all led the couple in the "dance of life." Next, the sponsors, godparents, aunts, uncles, and cousins led the bride and groom in that dance, called the *kalamatiano* (kah-

lah-ma-tee-ah-NO). Friends and family who were watching the dancers threw coins and bills onto the dance floor. You know what? The money was in honor of the couple, but not for them. At the end of the dance, all the children scrambled to pick up the treasure. Elena and Tony each got a handful of money to keep.

At the reception we met people from all over the country and in all kinds of work . . . from shoemakers to college professors. Mrs. Pappas says Greeks have an independent streak and many of the early immigrants went into business for themselves. Education has been important to Greeks since long ago. Greek-American families have worked hard to provide their children with college educations so they could enter a profession.

As we left the party, each of us was given a little favor, candied almonds wrapped in pink tulle. One of Elena's aunts explained that they are a wish for the couple to have many children and a sweet life together. If Maria and George have a marriage as happy as their wedding day it ought to be just wonderful!

❦ 5 ❧
Receiving the Light

My mother got to go with Dad on a business trip to New York City, and I got to spend four days with Elena and her family. It was a busy time for them because it was their Easter celebration. Mom told me to be sure to behave.

When I came over on Thursday afternoon, the Pappas family was getting ready to dye hard-boiled eggs. Elena's dad, as the head of the household, dipped the first egg into the dark red dye. Grandmother Pappas said the red color represents the blood of Jesus. When Elena's mother agreed to let us dye some of the eggs in other colors, I could tell that Grandmother Pappas wasn't happy about breaking the tradition of having all red eggs. I wondered what we were going to do with all the eggs. We must have dyed about six dozen of them. Elena and I were colored from head to toe.

Grandmother Pappas used some of the eggs to

33

JERABEK ELEMENTARY SCHOOL
10060 AVENIDA MAGNIFICA
SAN DIEGO, CA 92131

decorate the special Easter bread she made. Just before each loaf was baked, she tucked a dyed egg into the dough so that the egg showed when the loaf came out of the oven.

On Friday evening I went to the church service with the family. At the end, all the people followed the priests out into the street, carrying candles. The line wound around the block and back again to the church. I had my own candle, and I watched very carefully to keep it from blowing out.

Saturday was a day of preparation. Elena and I spent the afternoon cleaning up her room and helping her mother prepare for the Easter feast.

At eleven o'clock that night we all went to the church. Soon the huge church was filled to overflowing. The crowd grew quiet as a chanter sang hymns from the choir loft. At exactly midnight, the lights of the church went out. It was as dark as can be. I was a little bit scared. Then from behind the screen in front of the altar, the priest appeared, holding a lighted candle. "*DEFTE LAVETE FOS* (DEL-te LA-ve-te fos)," he sang. "Receive the Light." He lit the candle of the assistant priest, who then lit the candles of ten altar boys. They went through the church lighting the candles of one person in each pew. As the light was passed from person to person the darkness went away and the church was glowing with light.

After the service we all went to the church social

hall for refreshments. There was cheese and fruit and olives and red Easter eggs, and red wine for the grown-ups. It was a happy time. People were calling *CHRISTOS ANESTI* (kree-STOS-ah-NEH-stee)—Christ is risen—to each other and answering *ALETNOS ANESTI* (ah-lee-THOS-ah-NEH-stee)—Truly He is Risen.

We all had fun trying to see who had the strongest eggs. Elena said, "Let me see your egg." I held the red egg up, and she knocked her egg against mine and cracked it. "Aha!" she laughed, "now you try." I picked another egg from a plate on the table, held it tight and knocked her egg as hard as I could. *My* egg cracked! "Ha!" she cried, "I've got a champion egg." She went around to her family cracking everybody's eggs with her "lucky" egg until finally her cousin Tony cracked it with his egg. I had been sleepy in church, but now I was wide awake. It's a good thing, too, because there was more to come.

When we went home there was a feast waiting for us. We had roast lamb, a delicious soup called *mageretsa* (ma-yeh-REE-tsah), more red eggs, and of course the Easter bread. As we ate, Mr. Pappas asked his mother how she liked the service at church. Do you know, this is the first year she had ever attended. It used to be that only men attended the Easter service. The women stayed home and prepared the meal—and waited for the men to return. She had done that all these years. Now her face lit up as she thought about the service.

It was nearly four o'clock in the morning when we got to bed, so I slept until noon. When I came downstairs, I saw my parents were home. Elena and I gathered up some more eggs and took them to my mom and dad. I had so much to tell them! My parents wanted to go back over to the Pappas' house to thank them for keeping me. Would you believe it? We all ate some more red Easter eggs. Now I knew why we'd dyed so many. I patted my stomach. I thought if I ate one more egg I'd begin to cluck! It had been a wonderful celebration of Easter . . . one I would never forget.

❧ 6 ❧
Festival Time!

Jenny's here! In Baltimore! I'm so excited I can hardly stand it!

About six o'clock Friday evening Jenny and her parents pulled into our driveway. I ran out to meet them, followed by my mom and dad. There were hugs and kisses all around.

After they got settled in, I showed Jenny around the neighborhood. I had hoped the Pappas family would be home, but they were all out helping to get ready for the Greek Festival that's on this weekend. That night Jenny and I talked and talked until Mom reminded us we'd better get to sleep. Jenny went right off, but I lay there for a while wondering how she'd feel about Elena. Jenny was my best friend forever, but Elena was my best friend for now. I wasn't sure it was possible to have two best friends.

Saturday was a beautiful day, and I took Jenny to the Greek Festival. We got there about two o'clock and headed straight for the food booths. I got a Greek sausage, which is like a big hot dog, with fried onions and green peppers on it. Jenny got a *gyro* (YEE-ro), a sandwich made of meat that is cooked by turning it around and around like a top.

Then we bought some *loukomathes* (loo-koo-MAH-thehs). While we ate we watched a group of young people who were dressed in Greek costumes perform traditional dances in the church courtyard.

Mom and Jenny's mother were buying some hand-made Greek jewelry at one of the booths. Jenny and I wandered up and down the street "window shopping" at the gaily decorated booths. I kept looking for Elena. I was getting nervous about her meeting Jenny.

After a while we went inside the church. In one room there was a Greek grocery. It was just like a real store with big containers of olives, chunks of feta and kasseri (ka-SEH-ree) cheese, gallon cans of olive oil, pistachio nuts, and different kinds of pasta. On one table were loaves of homemade bread and the flat pita bread that is so good for making sandwiches.

Next to the grocery was a bakery. Yum! It was crammed full of the most delicious cookies and cakes you ever saw! There were *finikia* (fee-NEE-kee-ah), *xalva* (hal-VAH), *saragli* (sa-ra-GLEE), *kataifi* (kah-tah-EE-fee), and *kourambiethes* (koo-ram-BEH-thehs). I wanted to buy some of everything.

Still no Elena! I hoped she wasn't purposely avoiding us.

At six o'clock we met our parents outside the gymnasium door where people were waiting to buy tickets for dinner. A sample plate of each of the selections sat on the ticket table. I chose the *souvlaki* (soo-VLA-kee) platter and Jenny decided to have the *pastitsio* (pah-STEETS-see-o) plate.

The gym had been transformed from a basketball court to a lovely restaurant, with Greek columns and grape arbors. Small Greek flags fluttered from the ceiling overhead. When we were seated I saw Elena waiting on a table across the room. She had on such a pretty costume. In a few minutes she came over to our table, and I introduced her to Jenny and her family. She smiled politely and said it was nice to meet them. Then she said she had to get back to her table and hurried across the room.

"Is that the Greek girl you wrote to me about?" asked Jenny. I said that it was and that I thought she'd like her. I hoped with all my heart they'd get along all right.

After dinner we went to the large hall that was set up as a taverna. A *bouzouki* (boo-ZOO-kee) band was playing and there were lots of tables and chairs around the dance floor. The Pappas family joined us and before long they had everyone dancing. You should have seen my mom and dad and Jenny's folks doing the *hasapiko* (hah-SAH-pee-ko). Mrs. Pappas is a great dancer, so we all just followed her. Did we have fun!

When we sat down, Elena whispered something to

her mother and then came over to our side of the table. "Mother says you and Jenny can sleep over at our house tonight if you want and it's okay with your folks," she said. I looked at Jenny. "You want to?" I asked. "Sure," she replied, "that sounds great." Our parents agreed, so it was settled. Elena grinned and clapped her hands, then led us into one more dance before we left.

Later at the Pappas' house the three of us talked and laughed and played Uno until almost twelve. Finally, Mr. Pappas told us it was time to stop giggling and get to sleep. "*Kalinikta* (kal-lee-NEEXH-tah), girls," he said. "*Kalinikta*," we called back as we settled down in sleeping bags on the floor. The last thing I remember thinking as I closed my eyes was, "My best friend is Elena . . . and my other best friend is Jenny. Having two best friends is the greatest thing that ever happened to me."

Glossary

bouzouki (boo-ZOO-kee)—a stringed musical instrument, played with Greek songs and dances.

hasapiko (hah-SAH-pee-ko)—a Greek line dance.

icon (ee-KO-nah)—a representation in painting of a sacred personage.

kalimera (kah-lee-MEH-rah)—good morning.

kalinikta (kah-lee-NEEXH-tah)—good night.

kalispera (kah-lis-PEH-rah)—good evening.

kali tihi (kah-LEE TEE-hee)—good luck.

koukla (KOOK-lah)—a term of endearment; the Greek word for doll.

loukomathes (loo-koo-MAH-thehs)—fried puffs of dough dipped in honey.

pastitsio (pah-STEETS-see-o)—macaroni cooked with beef.

Piraeus (pee-reh-AHS)—the harbor near Athens.

taverna (tah-VERN-ah)—a Greek nightclub or tavern.

souvlaki (soo-VLA-kee)—lamb and vegetables broiled on a skewer.

yassou (YAH-soo)—a toast meaning "to your health," from the Greek words EÍS ΥΓEÍA.

Yia Yia (yah-YAH)—a Greek child's way of saying "Grandmother."

Some Books about Greece

D'Aulaire, Ingri and Edgar. *D'Aulaires' Book of Greek Myths.* Garden City, N.Y.: Doubleday and Co., 1962.

Eliot, Alexander. *Life—World Library—Greece.* New York: Time—Life Books, 1968.

Fenton, Sophia Horvati. *Greece—A Book to Begin On.* New York: Holt, Rinehart, Winston, 1969.

Gianakoulis, Theodore. *The Land and People of Greece.* Philadelphia and New York: J. B. Lippincott Co., 1972.

Masters, Robert V. *Greece in Pictures.* New York: Sterling Publishing Co., 1980.

Nicolaidis-Karanikolas, Maria. "Eternal Easter in a Greek Village." *National Geographic,* December 1983, pp. 768–777.

Robinson, Charles A. *Ancient Greece—A First Book.* New York: Franklin Watts, 1984.

Zolotov, Charlotte. *A Week in Yoni's World: Greece.* New York: Crowell-Collier Press, 1969.

About the Author

Phyllis Stuckey Yingling is a teacher in Baltimore, Maryland. She has written articles and stories for educational and religious publications as well as stories for children's magazines such as *Highlights for Children, Ranger Rick,* and *Humpty Dumpty.* For an article about Jane Addams, she won the *Highlights for Children* Biography of the Year Award in 1984. An article about Mary Katherine Goddard, a notable Baltimorean and newspaper editor during the American Revolution, appeared in a recent issue of *Maryland Magazine.* She lives in Baltimore with her husband, Carroll. Their children, Beth and Lewis (Chip), are married and establishing families of their own.